Experimental Band Aids

Sunday Banks

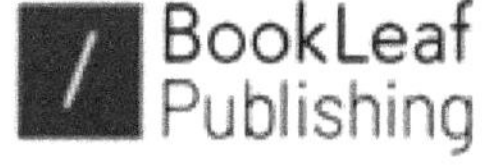

BookLeaf Publishing

Presentation by *BookLeaf Publishing*

Web: www.bookleafpub.com

E-mail: info@bookleafpub.com

ISBN: 9789358736120

First edition 2022

DEDICATION

For Lunetta Banks

ACKNOWLEDGEMENT

This book would not have existed without these amazing humans: Kaamilah Milton, Deborrah Sanchez, Erin Giacinto, Kevin Zuber, Else Eaton, and Tessa Kaigle. Thank you.

PREFACE

Someone I loved once gave me a box full of darkness. It took me years to understand that this too, was a gift.
— Mary Oliver

experiments

the first thing to go
was the taste of her lips
something I never cherished
fleeting like her lust for it
friendship is underrated
but young folks will always make a mess of it
the first thing I did
was succumb to the greed
a new experience, didn't open my eyes
a clear experiment, I daren't try
and why should I

If friends are for life
what does it matter, when feelings are involved
secrets and hushed tones
find a better way to die
a new experiment, true friendship
But it begins with deceit
Trust strung up and cut down
With hope to keep me leashed
once dead, reborn
a soul released, from it's locket

Unsettling

The head, it aches.
More pain it brings.
It nestles in.
It settles in.
Into my skin, nerves.
Into my skull, brain.
I think: how to end it, but that's just more pain.
I think; I should end it, but I couldn't fail again.
I must be certain, that it will be certain.
My feelings are often ignored, but mostly
unsettling.

Paranoid King

Yes I'm Paranoid But Am I Paranoid Enough
Yes I'm Paranoid But Am I Enough
Yes, But I'm Paranoid, Am I Enough
Yes But. I'm.
Am I? Paranoid.
Enough!

Prince Arthur

would you lay hands on the one you love
have you
I abandoned my throne to live in commune
I do not know love

spill it's secrets, with a knife to my throat
I take my knife to your breast, you sigh

TELL ME WHY
you'd never confess

IF it were up to me I'd live in our first kiss
I serve you, my servant, that couldn't happen
a lost dream, a different world

I die in your breath

Royal, but a slave to you
You in servitude to all but me
Looks, a nod

Your words meant more than you know
You mean more than I know
What was written in the stars, will be
We know this

You felt it in our first kiss
Sucking out my soul for confirmation
Or Narcissism

I died in your breath
yet mulled around the castle
FEAR

Heartbreaker

I'm Chasing Coral
First come; First served
You got my back, I got yours

Tell me did you mean it
Did you really care?
Did you really love me?
Tell me you didn't lie

Maybe one day I'll believe you
If only it would come
If only you would try

Such a strong willed woman
You probably set me up to die
Even if not knowing it

But you probably knew this
Planned it even
Sealed with a kiss, a touch, a flame
You knew what you were doing

In the end, you got what you wanted

Love

we are doomed
cursed
by the ones that made us
and those that made them

To repeat their mistakes
Even when we know them
Even though we can name them
Even if we don't claim them

History repeats

Children are eventual
Divorce is probable
War is imminent
Change is not growth
Subtle differences aren't unbreaking
The chain has been made
It must be destroyed in the process
Not polished, revamped, reconstructed

but you do you

Humans are animals too

Songs

OWIE
it hurts so badly
I jumped just when you said you'd catch me
but you took three steps to the left
arms out wide talking about you got me
saw the doubt in my eyes
told me not to be surprised
after all this is just the way that life goes
shrug it off, I suppose

lofi hiphop

Okay google
How can i help you
Play some relaxing sounds
Like ounces in a pound

CC: Everyone

"I forgot i locked the door"
Mine hands are cold
Will it snow please
Look at them
As they rejoice with entertainment
At mother nature's punishment
I suppose as only one should
If they at least knew or understood
The repercussions of themselves and others
Past future and present
Including my self
Smoking cigarettes for my health

Chasing Land

Chasing Ice Saved My Life
i'm sorry i meant it changed it
It's a fucking beautiful film
Have you ever seen it
If not i hope you do
i mean you are living
So i hope you care
To be hopeful
In a careless world
A universe
Upon universes
We've explored beyond our tech
But not our capacity
And that is not a lie based upon evolution
A universe under our feet
Taken for granted
A world of bees
Might as well be aliens overseas
Far out of reach
Over produced
Killed because it's possible
No difference between the dirt and the air
Not with your care
"I don't understand it's just hair"
But i'm an alien overseas
There's only seas

Tricks of the trade
But did you land it

Justice

you have my consent
no need to keep undressing me with your eyes
use your hands, feel between my thighs
take a sip, tell me again
now, my wine isn't perfectly suited for your
mind
leave me breathless
give me air
make me sweat
running your fingers through my hair
don't leave me
alone, when you're done
don't tease me, you were
just having fun

JUST JUST JUST
 BE There
PULL UP, YOU SQUARE

Aries Rising

I stalked a pigeon
as I thought about what you would say
Remembering I no longer care
as I thought about your reassurances
Figuring you never cared
But that isn't true, is it
Still it's not the same
Isn't it.

Withholding information is lying.
Especially when asked directly,
White lies are still lies.
I hate it.

Because you were always my favorite.
Smooth, cunning, anxious with anticipation.
Cocky with success.
I loved it.

Smiling with fear at your performances.

But I'm not a liar.
You know that's not true.
But we won't talk about it, just like we won't talk
about you.
To you, for you.

That's different, again.
No apologies for getting caught, only sorry for
any pain.

Are you?

Every lie I've told was wrapped up in you.
I remember the first, it still hurts.

It makes me hate me; Un-trustingly trustworthy.

And I hate liars, I could blame Spider-man.
But that's just a projection.

Not unlike how you think of me. If at all.

Remembering how you told me not to.
But I'll never do as I'm told.

Sweet and Sour

To be in a place you don't belong

Born in a place that made you strong

Evil understands sweet and sour
From charm to manipulation
You'd think they waited instead of planned it
You'd thought they'd left with out implanting

A little sugar goes a long way
But can't be appreciated without
That first bitter taste
But the bitter doesn't go away

People don't change. They grow.

Sweet and Sour.

The mean thirst for power
The hurt thirst for life

The hopeful and enraged must create the
lemonade they won't get to taste.

ErrAnds

I do not lack confidence
I'm just not cocky, attempts to be humble
But make no mistake
Trust me when I tell you, I have quite the ego

Maybe it is me who is obsessed with me
Narcissism
Ask me again and I'll tell you the truth

A ride to the bank
A ride to fill up the tank
Dark mornings to work
Bright afternoons to the beach

The first person you thought of
Was it not me

Never, ever
It was not me

however always me

I remember wanting to die before you,
And so I did

You always held me so close,

Wore me like my worn out backpack
Baggage rusted, filled with dust
I shake it off, rub it out
Attempts of removal, cleaning
It reforms, it's stuck
Unlike a scab, this is healing

don't let perfection be your downfall

Remember it's not your life, it's your liver

Hello again, did you miss me
Between errands
Would you help me run an errand

forgetmenot

fear will kill fate
uplifted with hate
could you try a little harder, maybe
kill me with your kiss
save me without your cape

you'd like that
over and over
unconditionally undying

forgive me or don't
forget me, you won't

I'd never forget your fingers in my palm
you were both drunk
I stood attempting to remain calm
in front of your family

I looked to the stars
ran away inside
confused
you didn't understand
I'd swear this was a setup

I'd swear you set me up
push it to the side

take your hand from mine

lay down, I need to sleep
but I can't sleep
crashing hard how you looked at me

wake up
do you even remember
did you actually forget
was it added to your list

What The Fuck Do You Even Call It

leave me be for awhile
even when I'm gone
nerves shot, blood clots
Forget Me, or not

The Tower

I left the door open for you
But you, you never came through

As I waited so patient
I grew bitter, impatient
Upset that others tried to get through
When I'm here waiting just for you

To reach my door they must have been blessed
To meet my shotgun and their death
A stack of bodies at my door
That I left open

Open for you
And still yet so many more dare it
Each and every one of them
Dead at the door
At my door, that I left open

I left the door open
For you to come through
But you never came
Suppose I lost, my way, fucks sake

Cause even though I left my door open
No one can get in

The open door is no more
Blocked by the bodies that came before

Suppose I like it, this way, fucks sake

There's no more waiting
Yet in the night I'll tell myself
I left the door open for you
It's up to you to come through

unfortunate things

you are destined for the most blessed
and yet so unfortunate
parts of life, things within moments
moments that last years, lifetimes
and generations.

love can be debilitating
to fall out and die on their grave
if that were forever

to lose a mother, a father, a friend
anyone!
over and over and over again
the heart can't take a day,
let alone multiple years
the time passes
Only Here
except it doesn't
Any Where

we are fated for the most cursed
and yet so hopeful
spaces of mind
between family or friends, enemies, the world
but most devotedly ourselves
over and over

but we move forward
ever so slowly
it becomes rapid
within our minds
never in time
forever out of place

May

enjoy the view
apple of my eye
enjoy the taste
rose water
on your tongue
shuffle the deck
open your lungs
now kill them
darlings
it's all yours
my life
my name
the cards are spread
do you WANT to play
the weather's nice
you say
Happy Birthday
that was last month
it's your turn now
reap the spoils
OUR love is never soiled
even in the soil
what we made
is everlasting
magic numbers
Golden Keys

we don't really drink
but we do spend

Open Mic

Off the top of my dome
Gonna tell you about my first home
The Ogontz public library
Where I'd wander and get lost
For hours, days, weeks
Forgetting to drink water
Forgetting to breathe
Learning every second
Watching every moment
Other kids: violence and porn
Adults gossip forlorned
But I'm ecstatic in heartbreak
On the edge of my seat with grief
I smile when I'm angry
And find a corner when I'm sad
My brother wants to join in
We're happy
But kids having too much fun learning
Makes some adults mad
They don't recognize him
They think he's another brat
They make him leave, he won't come back
I'm not upset, I'm disappointed
I thought humans were better than that
Back to my books
And my favorite librarian

She's sorry for the others
She's helpful and caring
Fifteen plus years later
I'll meet her again at Erie
When I come back home
And I'll cry in her presence
As an adult forlorned
She hugs me
The world never got better
But it's still our home

Keanu Reeves

light a candle
say a prayer
i'm Keanu Reeves, now
do you love me?

swallow, swallow
choke and cough
on it, what were you feeling
what's overthinking

apply clarity
square up against tom cruise
i'm not talking to myself
i'm raging against me

i was trying to honor You
me, Keanu Reeves
now, do you trust me?

two half truths and a lie
but it's on me to decide
i'll always choose love
forever, live or die.

bandages

sometimes you have to rip them off
sometimes you like to peel it slow

sometimes you can't let go

sometimes you choose
sometimes you won't

under time, over space

another, not yourself
only ever yourself

within your body, bone and spirit

within your thoughts
within your mind

this is the theme, this is the life

let it go, but don't
let it go